Cambridge **Discovery Education**™

▶ **INTERACTIVE READERS**

Series editor: Bob Hastings

UP IN THE AIR
OUR FIGHT AGAINST GRAVITY

B1+

Caroline Shackleton and Nathan Paul Turner

CAMBRIDGE
UNIVERSITY PRESS

Discovery
EDUCATION

CAMBRIDGE UNIVERSITY PRESS
Cambridge, New York, Melbourne, Madrid, Cape Town,
Singapore, São Paulo, Delhi, Mexico City

Cambridge University Press
32 Avenue of the Americas, New York, NY 10013-2473, USA

www.cambridge.org
Information on this title: www.cambridge.org/9781107634701

First published 2014

Printed in Hong Kong, China, by Golden Cup Printing Company Limited

A catalog record for this publication is available from the British Library.

Library of Congress Cataloging-in-Publication Data

Shackleton, Caroline.
  Up in the air : our fight against gravity / Caroline Shackleton and Nathan Paul Turner.
    pages cm. -- (Cambridge discovery interactive readers)
  ISBN 978-1-107-63470-1 (pbk. : alk. paper)
  1. Gravity--Juvenile literature. 2. English language--Textbooks for foreign speakers. 3. Readers
(Elementary) I. Title.

QC178.S463 2013
629.13--dc23

2013025106

ISBN 978-1-107-63470-1

Additional resources for this publication at www.cambridge.org

Layout services, art direction, book design, and photo research: Q2ABillSMITH GROUP
Editorial services: Hyphen S.A.
Audio production: CityVox, New York
Video production: Q2ABillSMITH GROUP

Contents

Before You Read:
Get Ready!

Humans have always looked for ways to reach the sky. Today we fly for transportation and scientific knowledge, to save lives, but also for sport and entertainment.

Words to Know

Look at the pictures. Then complete the sentences below with the correct words.

glider   jet   parachute

rocket   runway   wing

1 A _____ is a place where planes take off and land.

2 A _____ is a fast plane with a special engine that uses hot air and gases to push the airplane forward.

3 A _____ is an aircraft without an engine which flies using the air and the wind.

4 A _____ is one of two long, flat things that help a plane fly.

5 A _____ is like a plane that can travel in space.

6 A _____ is a large piece of cloth that helps you drop safely from a plane.

4

Read the paragraph. Then complete the definitions below with the correct highlighted words.

Years ago, people believed that man could never fly because of the force of gravity. But these days anyone can book a commercial flight on the Internet. Flying today is easy and comfortable. Because the air pressure on planes is the same as on the ground, passengers feel like they are traveling on a bus or train, even though they are flying at altitudes of thousands of meters.

1 _____ : the height above sea level

2 _____ : related to business; done for money

3 _____ : the power that makes things fall to the ground

4 _____ : the way air fills a space, which changes at different heights

CHAPTER 1

Gravity

THE FORCE OF GRAVITY IS STOPPING YOU
FROM FLOATING AWAY INTO THE AIR RIGHT NOW!

Gravity is all about attraction. Sometimes called "the law of attraction," gravity was discovered in the 17th century. Although scientists' understanding of gravity has become richer since then, the basic idea is still the same: the bigger the **object**, the more the objects around it are attracted to it. This means, for example, that our planet Earth is held in place by its attraction to the much larger Sun.

Gravity gives us weight and keeps our feet on the ground. For humans, the strength of gravity on Earth means that we can walk, run, or jump, but we cannot fly. And yet, perhaps because of the beauty of flying birds, or perhaps because of our curiosity about the Sun, the Moon, and the stars, humans have often looked up into the sky and dreamed of flying.

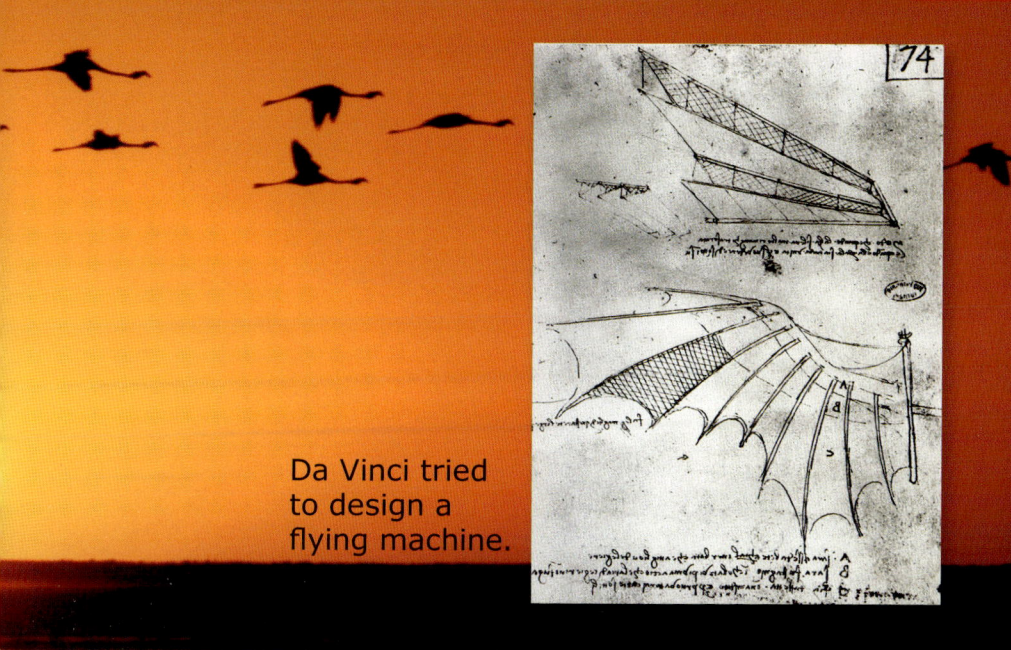

Da Vinci tried to design a flying machine.

By watching how birds fly and trying to copy them, scientists gradually learned about the physics of flying. One of the earliest thinkers to look seriously at flying was the 15th-century Italian artist and scientist Leonardo Da Vinci. Da Vinci made drawings for three different types of flying machines. One was similar to a modern glider, another worked like a helicopter, and the third was a type of parachute.

Although Da Vinci's inventions were never built in his lifetime, we now know that at least one of his designs works. In 2000, Da Vinci's parachute design was built and tested by an expert parachute jumper, Adrian Nichols. Nichols made a jump from 3,000 meters and landed perfectly. He even found that the parachute made from Da Vinci's design flew more smoothly than a modern parachute!

A big problem for designing flying machines was finding out how to lift them into the air. Many of the first ideas were based on birds, with machines that used moving wings to try to take off! Birds' bodies, however, are light and their wings are strong, so it was impossible to make a machine that flew like a bird.

But there was another way to create lift. The idea of filling a bag with hot air had been used by the Chinese for centuries for sending messages. In the 18th century, Europeans began to experiment with balloons for carrying people.

In 1783, in France, the Montgolfier brothers made the first successful hot air balloon for passengers. It worked by heating the air inside a paper and silk balloon. The brothers, however, were not sure that flying was safe for people, so the passengers in the first flight were animals: a sheep, a duck, and a rooster.

Unlike lighter-than-air balloons, machines still had the problem of getting off the ground. Steam[1] engines were just too heavy. But in 1885 Karl Benz gave aircraft designers new hope.

[1] **steam:** the gas that water makes when you heat it to 100° C

? **UNDERSTAND**

Why were the first flying experiments unsuccessful?

His invention, the gasoline engine, was light enough to fly. A few gas-powered planes were built. Unfortunately, all of them crashed. Now the problem was that they were too difficult to control.

It took two bicycle mechanics from Ohio, USA, to solve the problem. Brothers Wilbur and Orville Wright had been fascinated by flying machines for years. They used their skills as mechanics to make and fly gliders. This allowed them to perfect the controls a pilot needs to fly a plane.

They added an engine to their glider to create the *Wright Flyer I*. On December 17, 1903, they made the first successful powered flight and changed history forever.

CHAPTER 2

Air Transportation

THE 20TH CENTURY MAY WELL BE LOOKED BACK ON AS THE AGE OF FLIGHT.

After the Wright brothers' invention in 1903, the airplane quickly **developed** into an important means of transport and communication, changing the way we experience and see our world.

Helicopters, balloons, and parachutes, and later the development of space rockets, also took flying to new heights. The airplane, however, is probably the first thing that comes to mind when you think about flying.

In the last 50 years, airplanes have become the usual way to travel long distances. The first airplanes, however, were used more to carry objects, not passengers. One of the first uses for planes was the US airmail service, carrying letters and parcels[2] across the United States.

[2] **parcel:** something sent by post in a box

In 1914, the first commercial passenger flight took place in the USA. Only one passenger bought a seat! By 1919, there were international passenger flights between London and Paris.

Long distance international passenger services didn't become common until after World War II. In 1952, the first jet plane for passengers, the de Havilland 106, flew from London to Johannesburg, South Africa. It carried just 36 passengers and took 24 hours to complete the journey, stopping five times on the way.

The first transatlantic jet service between London and New York started in 1958. It took just over ten hours. Over the next decade,[3] jet planes got bigger and faster. One of the most popular was the Boeing 747. First introduced in 1968 and still in use today, the 747 can carry as many as 600 passengers!

[3] **decade:** a period of ten years

In 1947 a US Air Force plane, the Bell X-1, broke the sound barrier – went faster than the speed of sound. It wasn't until 1976, however, that supersonic[4] flight became a reality for passengers. The Concorde jet could fly 2,450 kilometers an hour, carrying 100 passengers from London or Paris to New York in just four hours, reaching **altitudes** of 50,000 kilometers!

Although it was noisy and expensive, the Concorde became famous as the plane of choice for the rich and famous. However, after an accident near Paris in July 2000, when all its passengers and crew died, worries grew about the jet's safety. In May 2003, the Concorde landed in New York for the last time.

Today, the focus of airplane designers is to make planes that are more environmentally friendly. The new Boeing 787 Dreamliner, for example, uses 20 percent less fuel than other large passenger planes.

[4]**supersonic:** faster than the speed of sound

The Concorde could fly faster than the speed of sound.

Another of Leonardo Da Vinci's amazing 15th-century designs for flying machines shows a machine without wings. Instead, it has long, thin blades[5] that spin in a circle very fast above the machine.

A search-and-rescue operation

Unfortunately, Da Vinci's machine was never built. It was only in 1939, thanks to the Russian inventor Igor Sikorsky, that the first helicopter flew into the sky. And just like in Da Vinci's design, Sikorsky's helicopter used spinning blades for lift and power.

Helicopters have one big advantage over airplanes. They don't need an expensive, well-kept runway to take off and land. Because they are highly maneuverable[6] and can take off and land almost anywhere, helicopters are often used in search-and-rescue operations. They have saved tens of thousands of lives.

[5]**blade:** a long, thin, flat piece of metal, like a knife
[6]**maneuverable:** easy to move and direct

Video Quest

Helicopters in Alaska

Watch this video about how helicopters are used in Alaska. What was this helicopter used for?

CHAPTER 3

Unusual Aircraft

FLOATING INTO THE RECORD BOOKS . . .

Although planes and helicopters are the most common flying machines in use today, they are, of course, not the only ones. Between the Montgolfier brothers' first flight in a hot air balloon and the Wright brothers' first successful plane flight, more than one hundred years passed and many interesting experiments were carried out.

In 1785, Jean Pierre Blanchard and John Jeffries flew a balloon across the English Channel. In the century that followed, balloons were used for both exploration and as lookout posts[7] in wars.

There were two main types of balloons. The first balloons heated the air in the balloon to make it expand[8] and rise. But soon, balloonists started to use lighter-than-air gases like helium and hydrogen inside the balloon to fly higher. Nowadays, both types of technology are still in use. Hot air balloons are more common, but many of the high altitude balloons use helium gas.

[7] **lookout post:** a good place to watch from
[8] **expand:** increase in size

The problem with early balloons was they were hard to control. In the 19th century, balloons were redesigned to create the first passenger airships. These "ships of the sky" had a long metal **frame** covered by material that was then filled with a lighter-than-air gas, normally hydrogen. Thanks to the invention of the gasoline engine, the ships could be easily controlled.

The first passenger airline was the German DELAG company, which started commercial airship flights in 1910. Germany also used airships in World War I to bomb British cities.

After the war, airships continued to be developed for military[9] and commercial purposes. However, the hydrogen gas they used was highly **explosive**, and there were a number of terrible accidents. In 1937, the airship *Hindenburg* caught fire while trying to land in New Jersey, USA. Thirty-six people died. It was the end of commercial hydrogen airships.

[9]**military:** related to soldiers and armies

The famous *Hindenburg* accident

?
ANALYZE
When might an airship be better than an airplane? Why?

The Goodyear Blimp

Although travel in commercial airships with solid frames was stopped after the *Hindenburg* accident, a similar type of airship, known as a blimp, is still made and flown to this day. While the cigar-shaped balloon looks similar to the old solid-frame airships, the blimp's balloon body has no frame and is kept in shape by air **pressure**. The gas used in the balloon is helium, which is not explosive like hydrogen, and therefore not as dangerous.

In total, there are fewer than 50 blimps in the world today. The most famous modern-day example of a blimp is probably the Goodyear Blimp, made by the Goodyear Tire and Rubber Company since 1925 and used for advertising. Because of its large size and slow speed, the blimp can be easily seen floating above cities with its huge Goodyear sign on the side of the balloon.

Thanks to their ability to fly to high altitudes, balloons have **set many world records**. As early as 1783, just months after the first balloon flight, Jean-François Pilâtre de Rozier flew to a height of four kilometers.

By 1862, Henry Coxwell and James Glaisher had set a world record at a height of 9,144 meters. The problems at such a high altitude are the cold, low air pressure, and lack of oxygen. Coxwell suffered frostbite[10] and Glaisher actually became unconscious.[11]

In 1927, Captain Hawthorne Gray set a new record of 13,222 kilometers. Tragically, Gray died during the flight when his oxygen ran out. The oxygen problem was finally solved by the use of pressurized cabins, allowing balloons to rise higher and higher. This cabin technology helped prove that humans could live in a low-pressure environment, and led to the pressurized cabins necessary for commercial air travel and space flight.

[10] **frostbite:** when cold damages the body, especially the fingers and toes
[11] **unconscious:** not able to see or feel things; not awake

Video Quest

Reduced Gravity Program

Watch this video about astronauts training for a space walk. How do they practice being without gravity?

Wing walking on biplanes

CHAPTER 4

Fun in the Air

HOBBY FLYING AND OTHER ACTIVITIES IN THE AIR ARE BECOMING MORE POPULAR.

The first person to try "wing walking" didn't do it for fun. He was Ormer Locklear, a young American pilot, who stepped out onto the wing of his biplane during World War I to fix a mechanical problem. Locklear did it again at an air show in 1918, and in the 1920s it became very popular for flyers to perform tricks on the wings of their plane while flying through the sky.

Wing walking is still practiced today. No training is necessary as long as the wing walker is safely tied to the wing, so wing walking flights are often offered as special gifts. In 2009, an eight-year-old boy became the youngest person to wing walk. Tiger Brewer stepped out onto the wing of his grandfather's biplane while it was flying at 160 kilometers per hour to set the world record.

Leonardo Da Vinci designed the first parachute, but the modern parachute dates from the late 18th century. Originally designed as safety equipment for pilots, parachutes are now used for fun. Parachuting and skydiving are practiced by people of all ages. It

Skydivers jump, fall, and then open their parachute.

may seem dangerous, but it's quite safe. In the USA, there is about one death for every 15,000 parachute jumps, so the risk of dying while parachuting is only about 0.0007 percent!

BASE jumping, however, is dangerous. It is about 40 times riskier than parachuting from a plane. BASE jumpers parachute from high places: from the tops of buildings or monuments (even when they're not allowed to), from skyscrapers[12] that

BASE jumping from Angel Falls

are still being built, and from mountains and cliffs. One of the most amazing BASE jumps is the jump from Angel Falls in Venezuela, the world's highest waterfall.

[12] **skyscraper:** a very tall building

Video Quest

BASE jumping

Watch this video about a BASE jumper in Alaska. Why is the landing so dangerous?

Hang gliding

Before the invention of gasoline motors, the only planes were gliders. They were often launched[13] from hillsides and controlled by moving the pilot's weight from side to side. Modern gliders have much more control and are towed[14] into the air by another plane or by a ground vehicle or machine. When the glider is moving quickly enough, it is freed and the pilot **glides** on warm air to rise high in the sky.

In the 1960s, some people began flying a new kind of small glider off the tops of hills. The sport is called hang gliding because the pilot hangs from a frame below the glider. In 2012, Dustin Martin and Jonny Durand flew their hang gliders for an incredible 761 kilometers to set a new distance record.

[13]**launch:** send a vehicle out, e.g., a plane into the air or a ship onto water
[14]**tow:** pull a boat, aircraft, or other vehicle using a rope tied to another vehicle

In the 1980s some hang gliders thought of gliding with parachutes. The sport is now known as paragliding and has become popular around the world.

One of the advantages of paragliding is that the parachute has no frame, so it can be easily packed into a bag and carried. Also, the slow flying speeds mean that – with the right training and equipment – it is a very safe form of flying.

Flights in paragliders can last several hours. In 2008, the South African pilot Nevil Hulett set a world record for the longest flight in a paraglider. He flew at an altitude of over 5,000 meters for the incredible distance of 502.2 kilometers! But now, some paragliders use motors to help them fly even longer distances. The world record for a motorized paraglider stands at an amazing 1,105 kilometers.

Paragliding

Wingsuit flying is a much more dangerous sport. It's a terrifying mixture of parachuting and paragliding. The wings are part of a special suit that allows the brave (or foolish) flyer to glide through the air. The wings are very small, however, and a wingsuit flyer cannot fly slowly enough to land safely. Instead, the final part of the flight is made using a traditional parachute.

Wingsuit flyers either dive from planes or from the top of very high mountains, a type of BASE jumping known as WiSBASE. One of the most dangerous forms of this sport is when jumpers try to fly down mountainsides while keeping as close as possible to the ground at high speeds, a style known as proximity diving. This practice has led to a number of deaths.

Wingsuit flying

There are other activities that give a feeling of flying – or just falling! For example, in bungee jumping, people tie themselves to a strong rubber cord and jump from bridges or towers that are hundreds of meters high. At the bottom of the "flight" the rubber cord stops their fall and bounces them back up into the air.

Bungee jumping

The highest bungee jump in the world is from the Royal Gorge Bridge, Colorado, USA. At 321 meters, this jump reaches a falling speed of almost 180 kilometers per hour!

A roller coaster

Another, safer way of getting a feeling of flying is to go on an amusement ride, like a roller coaster. The world's fastest roller coaster is the Formula Rossa at Ferrari World in Abu Dhabi. Passengers ride in Formula 1-style cars and reach speeds of 240 kilometers per hour in only four seconds!

?

EVALUATE

List the sports in this chapter in the order of how dangerous you think they are. Give your reasons.

CHAPTER 5

What Do You Think?

THERE ARE LOTS OF WEBSITES SELLING ADVENTURE GIFTS.

If you could get an exciting gift, would you choose a ride in a hot air balloon, to parachute from a plane, or even to wing walk? What about lessons to learn how to fly a helicopter?

Look at these advertisements and decide which ones you would like to do and why. Which ones would you definitely not like to try? Why not?

A Balloon Ride

Fly gently through the sky in a hot air balloon to see amazing views. Would you choose to fly over mountains or along the coast?

Cost: $$$
Safety: very safe
Duration: half a day including a one-hour flight

A Parachute Jump

Imagine standing in the doorway of an aircraft flying at 3,000 meters – falling into the clouds, diving down through the air at over 193 kilometers per hour! Could you do it?

Cost: $$$$
Safety: sometimes problems when landing
Duration: half a day including a 20-minute jump

Wing Walking

Give your family and friends a show they will never forget. You will learn a short, 10-minute performance, and you can invite up to 50 people to watch. Who would you invite to see the performance?

Cost: $$$$$
Safety: need safety equipment
Duration: half a day including a 10-minute flight

Fly a Helicopter

Helicopter flying lessons. 30 minutes flying a helicopter over the place of your choice. Where would you go?

Cost: $$
Safety: safe in most places
Duration: 30-minute flight

Fly a Jet Plane

Speed down the runway in a real fighter jet. You can fly a real fighter jet – even if you have never flown a plane! Would you like to be a pilot?

Cost: $$$$$$$$$$$$$$$$$$$
Safety: you can't be afraid of high speeds
Duration: whole day

A Bungee Jump

You're standing on a bridge hundreds of meters above a river. You have a rubber cord around your ankle and a nervous feeling in your stomach. Will you jump or will someone have to push you?

Cost: $
Safety: possible eyesight damage
Duration: six seconds

After You Read

Read the sentences and choose Ⓐ, Ⓑ, Ⓒ, or Ⓓ.

1 Why was it difficult to model flying machines on birds?
- Ⓐ Machines could not copy the shape of birds' wings.
- Ⓑ Scientists did not know how birds fly.
- Ⓒ The machines were too heavy.
- Ⓓ Bird's wings move too fast.

2 Who were the first air passengers?
- Ⓐ Leonardo Da Vinci and a friend
- Ⓑ Some Chinese inventors
- Ⓒ The Montgolfier brothers
- Ⓓ Some animals

3 What did the Wright brothers invent?
- Ⓐ The gasoline engine
- Ⓑ A new kind of bicycle
- Ⓒ The first motorized plane
- Ⓓ The first glider

4 What is the main focus of airplane designers nowadays?
- Ⓐ To reduce flying time
- Ⓑ To reduce negative environmental effects
- Ⓒ To reach higher and calmer altitudes
- Ⓓ To become faster and bigger

5 Why did the *Hindenburg* catch fire in 1937?
- Ⓐ Its hydrogen gas was very explosive.
- Ⓑ It reached too high an altitude.
- Ⓒ Its helium gas was very explosive.
- Ⓓ It crashed into an airplane.

6 Why are blimps used nowadays?

  (A) Because they are easy to make
  (B) Because they use a non-explosive gas
  (C) To help sell things
  (D) For holidays

7 Why did the first person walk on the wing of a plane?

  (A) To start a new sport
  (B) To introduce a new hobby
  (C) To entertain people
  (D) To make some repairs

8 How is paragliding a better sport than parachuting?

  (A) The equipment is easier to transport.
  (B) The motor in a paraglider is easy to use.
  (C) It doesn't need a lot of training.
  (D) It is much safer in bad weather.

True or False?

Read the sentences and write T (True) or F (False).

1 _____ Big things have a greater force of gravity.

2 _____ Leonardo Da Vinci built the first parachute.

3 _____ Technology for lifting things into the air was first used in the 18th century.

4 _____ The first commercial jet flight took one day to complete.

5 _____ Helicopters have saved tens of thousands of lives.

6 _____ Hydrogen gas made airships dangerous.

7 _____ Blimps get their shape from a solid frame.

8 _____ You need to do a course to learn how to wing walk.

9 _____ BASE jumping is based on parachuting.

10 _____ Wingsuit flyers use a parachute to take off.

Answer Key

Words to Know, page 4

① runway **②** jet **③** glider **④** wing **⑤** rocket **⑥** parachute

Words to Know, page 5

① altitude **②** commercial **③** force of gravity
④ air pressure

Understand, page 9

They did not have enough scientific knowledge. It was impossible to make machines like birds.

Video Quest, page 13

A helicopter took repairmen and equipment to the place where an avalanche destroyed electricity transmission towers, leaving the town without electricity.

Analyze, page 15

Answers will vary.

Video Quest, page 17

They spend hours in a specially adapted plane, the KC135, which flies in short semicircles and dives down.

Video Quest, page 19

Because he lands on ice, and the ice is moving, he could easily land badly and fall into a hole.

Evaluate, page 23

Answers will vary.

Choose the Correct Answers, page 26

① C **②** D **③** C **④** B **⑤** A **⑥** C **⑦** D **⑧** A

True or False?, page 27

① T **②** F **③** F **④** T **⑤** T **⑥** T **⑦** F **⑧** F **⑨** T **⑩** F